PERFORMING A...

THE
ESS...

RAILWAY

NEW

CLOTHES

A PLAY...

WIL...L

SAMUEL FRENCH

LONDON
NEW YORK TORONTO SYDNEY HOLLYWOOD

THE RAILWAYMAN'S NEW CLOTHES

A small, suburban branch shop of a multiple men's outfitters. There is a central counter, a fitting cubicle, a cashier's desk. A glass-fronted door leads to the street outside. Rolls of cloth are stacked on shelves underneath the counter. There are ready-to-wear suits on racks round the walls. Shirts and ties are on display

As the CURTAIN *rises, Hartigan, the shop assistant, is blocking a roll of cloth on the counter. Lumley, the branch manager, watches him sourly for a moment*

Lumley Mr Hartigan! I say, Mr Hartigan! You might make note, I say you might make note, that in future we will not come to business in suède shoes.

Hartigan No, Mr Lumley.

Lumley Or knitted ties.

Hartigan Sorry, sir.

Lumley Never "sir". The customer is "sir". We do try to allow him that prerogative. "Sir" or "madam" for the customer. You and I being neither of noble birth nor in possession of a life peerage are *Mr* Lumley and *Mr* Hartigan. I say, we're neither of us in possession of a life peerage, Mr Hartigan.

Hartigan No, Mr Lumley.

Lumley We may on occasion consider ourself better than the customer, but we allow them due deference because they *are* the customer. I say, we try to show them just that little bit of respect.

Charles and Edith Henshaw, a railway porter and his wife, enter the shop. Charles is wearing his uniform

Lumley is thus presented with an immediate opportunity for making his point with Hartigan. He rubs his hands together, unctuously

Lumley Good morning, *sir*. Good morning, *madam*.

And Lumley, having shown his customers just that little bit of respect, dismisses them into the hands of his assistant

Forward, Mr Hartigan.

Lumley steps back a couple of paces, pretending work, but keeping a watchful and distrusting eye on Hartigan's attempts at salesmanship. Hartigan approaches the Henshaws. He is new to his job and is unused to handling customers

Hartigan Good morning, sir. Good morning, madam.
Mrs Henshaw Well? Tell him.
Henshaw It's—er—about a suit.
Hartigan Off the peg or made to measure?

Henshaw glances at his wife, uneasily. Hartigan becomes aware of the cold stare and pursed lips of Lumley. Hartigan corrects himself

Were you intending a bespoke suit, sir, or are you contemplating something from our comprehensive range of ready-to-wear garments? (*He produces a pattern book of cloth pieces*) These are our new summer suitings, two-piece or three-piece, sir, to suit your own particular style and specifications and delivery is guaranteed within six weeks of the date of the order.

Mrs Henshaw We've not come here to look at patterns. (*To Henshaw*) Tell him—why you've come—standing there like a ventriloquist's dummy. (*To Hartigan*) He wants to cancel an order.

Henshaw That's right. I've come to cancel an order.

Hartigan does not know how to handle the situation and is aware of Lumley's eyes boring into the back of his neck

Oh, yes? A cancellation.

Mrs Henshaw He's been in before. He ordered a suit. He's changed his mind. He doesn't want it.

Lumley, seeing a commission slip through his fingers, sweeps across to take over

Lumley If I may, Mr Hartigan, I think I can take care of this customer.

Mrs Henshaw (*resenting the intrusion*) The young lad was trying.

Henshaw I think it was this gentleman who did serve me.

Lumley (*who does not remember Henshaw from Adam*) I thought
I recognized your face, Mister—er—er . . .

Henshaw Henshaw.

Lumley Henshaw, yes. I say, I had a feeling your face was
familiar.

Henshaw You measured me up for it.

*Lumley purses his lips again. He appraises Henshaw's body, up
and down—the face means nothing to him but his expert eye
remembers the figure*

Lumley Three-piece suit, one pair of trousers, button two jacket,
two inside pockets.

Mrs Henshaw He's come in to get back his deposit.

Lumley (*guilelessly*) Well now, that shouldn't prove difficult,
should it? I say, that shouldn't afford us too much trouble.
If I might trouble you, Mr Hartigan, the current order book?

Hartigan goes to the cashier desk

About a week ago would it be? When we first had the pleasure
of your company?

Henshaw It's more than that by a long chalk. Must be a month
ago at least.

Hartigan returns with the current order book

Lumley Of course! Of course! I recall the date exactly! Total
recall, Mr Henshaw. Late afternoon, I remember. Staff tea-
break. Approximately four-thirty.

Henshaw That'd be it. (*To Mrs Henshaw*) Because I was going
on early shift.

Lumley (*taking the order book*) Thank you, Mr Hartigan. (*He
makes a little joke, smirking at Mrs Henshaw*) The nominal roll,
Mrs Henshaw. And lo! Abou Ben Adam's name led all the
rest. (*The joke falls flat*) Quite.

Mrs Henshaw I didn't know he'd ordered a suit. That's how he
is. He keeps things to himself. (*To her husband*) Why didn't
you say you'd ordered a suit?

Henshaw shrugs, she turns back to Lumley

Last night, jigger me, he's having his tea, cool as you like, out it trots: "I've ordered a suit." (*Back to Henshaw*) Why couldn't you tell me in the first place?

Lumley, attempting to keep the peace, refers to the order book

Lumley Seek and ye shall find! Mr Henshaw, forty-two Agammemnon Drive, Lower Burtley. Three-piece, one pair of trousers, button two, jetted pockets, optional flaps.

Henshaw Brown?

Lumley Pattern number JY three-four-two. Brown check. Price of suit, thirty-five pounds seventy-five pence, deposit paid, two pounds fifty pence.

Henshaw (*to his wife*) It was all I had on me. Apart from odd coppers.

Mrs Henshaw Just so long as you get it back.

Lumley I do remember the occasion. Vividly. It is not general company practice to accept a deposit in default of twenty per cent of the total cost. We were prepared to bend the rules in your particular instance.

Mrs Henshaw Thirty-five pounds seventy-five for a suit to go pubbing in? Downright ridiculous.

Lumley A bespoke suit, Mrs Henshaw.

Mrs Henshaw looks blank

Made to measure.

Mrs Henshaw That's what I'm saying. What's he want made-to-measure for? He's never had made-to-measure in his life.

Lumley Am I to take it, Mrs Henshaw, that you would have no objection to, say, a choice of suiting for Mr Henshaw from our ample range of ready-to-wear garments?

Mrs Henshaw Well . . .

Lumley Mr Hartigan! Thirty-eight chest, stock size, YB three-six-two.

Hartigan goes to the ready-to-wear racks and hunts out a suit

Mrs Henshaw We only came in to get his deposit back.

Lumley The price of any purchase made from our comprehensive ready-to-wear range would, naturally, be defrayed by the amount advanced as a deposit for the bespoke garment. Two pounds fifty pence.

Mrs Henshaw rises, about to leave

Mrs Henshaw We'll have the money and think about it.

Mrs Henshaw picks up her gloves and handbag preparatory to walking out. But Lumley has his hands on the back of her husband's collar

Lumley If we could just slip the jacket off for a moment, sir? If it's no great inconvenience?

Henshaw allows Lumley to take off his uniform jacket and is thus prevented from leaving the shop. Hartigan approaches with a two-piece suit on a hanger. Lumley holds up Henshaw's porter's jacket in some surprise, as if he had just noticed it

British Railways, sir! I remember the old LMS very well. I say, I recall the old LMS with deep affection. (*He puts the jacket down and takes the suit from Hartigan*) Thank you, Mr Hartigan. (*He holds up the suit by the hanger and studies it with pride*) Now!

Mrs Henshaw I don't like that.

Henshaw It's blue.

Lumley It does have that distinction, yes, sir.

Mrs Henshaw I don't like that at all.

Lumley I'm not suggesting this particular suit, madam. Not at all. I'm only trying to ascertain the gentleman's size. Slip the jacket on, sir. Just for the size.

Henshaw allows Lumley to help him into the jacket. Lumley smooths the shoulders on the jacket and steps back, modestly proud, his hands clasped together

There! I go for the size and I'm right first time!

Henshaw (*with an apprehensive glance at his wife*) What do you think?

Lumley One moment, sir.

Lumley steps forward and fastens a front button. He smiles at Mrs Henshaw, looking for her approval. But Mrs Henshaw's mouth is shut tight, revealing nothing. She goes and runs a hand over the trousers which Lumley has placed on the counter

Mrs Henshaw It doesn't come with a waistcoat then?

Lumley Not at the give-away price, madam, no.

Mrs Henshaw How much did you say it was?

Lumley The Madison Avenue Executive suit, madam. Waist-fitting trouser, belt loops *and* brace attachments, button two jacket, *two* inside pockets.

Lumley glances casually at the price tag on the cuff of a sleeve and reacts with some surprise

Twenty-seven pounds! Remarkable value!

Mrs Henshaw He's always been used to a waistcoat.

Lumley That would be twenty-seven pounds less your original deposit, let me see, less two pounds fifty, twenty-four pounds only to be paid.

Mrs Henshaw He's always had three-piece. I like to see him in a waistcoat.

Lumley It's the trans-Atlantic style, of course. Extremely popular today.

Henshaw (*to his wife*) You're not sure then?

Mrs Henshaw Just turn round.

Henshaw obliges

Just turn round again.

Henshaw does as he is bid. Lumley invites him to make use of a full-length mirror

Lumley If you'd care to glance over your shoulder, sir, it would give you the opportunity of appraising the fitting across the back.

Henshaw (*to his wife*) You're not all that struck, are you?

Mrs Henshaw You stand like a sack of potatoes! Hold your shoulders back! God Almighty, Charles, just try and frame yourself!

Henshaw makes a half-hearted and embarrassed attempt at standing straight. Mrs Henshaw walks round him

Is it a bit tight—underneath the armpits?

Henshaw, his elbows bent, waggles his arms and looks rather like a cockerel

Henshaw No. No. It feels all right.

Mrs Henshaw It doesn't *look* all right. (*To Lumley*) It's not his fit.

Lumley steps forward and tugs the jacket down at the back

Lumley We do tend to find that the arm fittings are inclined to *ease* themselves in. I say, we prefer the customer to wear the garment for the odd occasion and let the suit adjust itself to him.

Mrs Henshaw How do you mean?

Lumley I say, rather than make any minor alterations, to the customer's final satisfaction, we'd rather he wore it for a week.

Mrs Henshaw If it doesn't fit him now, it won't fit him in a week's time.

Henshaw (*feeling underneath his armpits*) It *is* pulling a bit just under here, y'know.

Lumley Of course, the charge for minor alterations, if required, is purely nominal. I say, it's simply a matter of pence, not pounds.

Henshaw takes off the jacket, assisted by Lumley

Mrs Henshaw What have you got to show us in his size?

Lumley again appraises Henshaw's build, pursing his lips and shaking his head

Lumley There is one tiny obstacle to overcome in that Mr Henshaw tends towards putting on that little bit of weight.

Mrs Henshaw He's always been fitted off the peg.

Lumley *Has*, maybe. With respect, madam, you've placed your thumb on it. I'd venture to suggest that it's been some years, without intending offence, I say, it's been some years since you've been given complete satisfaction from a ready-to-wear suit?

Henshaw It's been a few years since I bought a suit, yes.

Lumley Ah! (*He pats his own waistline with both hands*) "Time, you old gypsyman, will you not stay? I say, put up your caravan just for one day." (*With an apologetic smile to Mrs Henshaw*) I wouldn't attempt to guarantee *complete* satisfaction, not from our ready-to-wear range.

Mrs Henshaw If you haven't got anything we'll just have to try somewhere else, that's all.

Lumley By all means, madam. It's your prerogative. But you'll come away empty-handed, madam, I'm very much afraid.

Henshaw There's that big shop in the centre of town. They always seem to have plenty of suits in the window.

Lumley Brightling and Sons, sir, yes. An exceedingly comprehensive store. Excellent range of merchandise. I've had recourse to recommend them to many of my customers on frequent occasions. Stock-size customers, of course.

Mrs Henshaw collects her belongings together again: gloves, handbag, shopping bag, etc.

Mrs Henshaw We'll have a walk up there then, Charles.

Lumley (*helping Henshaw into his railway jacket*) Allow me, sir. Yes, the old LMS, the old LNER—the GWR, which I recall I had the benefit of on many a highday and holiday. (*He buttons up the jacket*) There we are, sir.

Henshaw Thank you.

Lumley Not at all, sir. My pleasure entirely. Cheery-bye. Good day, madam.

Mrs Henshaw Good morning.

Mr and Mrs Henshaw move towards the door. Hartigan, surprised whispers to Lumley

Hartigan You've lost a customer!

Lumley (*also whispering*) I've got him, Mr Hartigan. I have him well and truly! (*Without pausing, he calls out to the Henshaws who have reached the door*) One moment, sir! I say, aren't we both forgetting something? The very purpose of your visit? The return of your deposit!

Mrs Henshaw glares at her husband, laying the blame on him, and strides back into the shop. Henshaw follows her. Lumley crosses to the cash desk

This way! My goodness me, we must send you on your way rejoicing! (*Calling across the shop*) Order book, if you please, Mr Hartigan!

Mrs Henshaw We know how much it was—it was two pounds fifty.

Hartigan hands Lumley the order book

Lumley (*jocularly*) Gracious, we're not denying liability! Thank you, Mr Hartigan. (*To Mrs Henshaw*) I say, we're not intending High Court procedure, madam! (*He locates the page in the order book*) Order number two-one-four-three, Mr Henshaw, C., cash deposit, two pounds fifty pence. It's purely a matter of keeping the branch books in order, Mrs Henshaw. (*He makes an entry in the order book*) I say, we're all accountable to Head Office, ma'am. Now, two pounds fifty . . .

Lumley opens the cash drawer and feigns surprise, finding it empty

Mr Hartigan?

Hartigan Yes, Mr Lumley?

Lumley (*to Mrs Henshaw; confidentially*) Mr Hartigan is another one whose head would fall off were it not attached to his body. (*To Hartigan*) You've neglected to go to the bank again.

Mrs Henshaw (*sensing difficulties*) Oh, yes?

Henshaw Nothing in the kitty?

Lumley Our cup doth not runneth over, Mr Henshaw. We have journeyed to the well and found it dry.

Henshaw Oh, dear.

Mrs Henshaw We'll have to traipse down here again then, that's all there is for it.

Henshaw I've got to go on shift, Edith.

Mrs Henshaw I shall call back myself then, this afternoon.

Lumley (*raising his hands in mock horror*) Perish the thought, madam! Totally unnecessary, I do assure you! (*He produces his wallet with a flourish*) I think I can trust the company with an advance of two pounds fifty from my own pocket. I say, I think Head Office assets will cover such an amount—at any rate, I shan't lose sleep. I can promise you that! (*He takes two pound notes from his wallet and lays them on the cash desk*)

Henshaw You're sure it's no inconvenience?

Lumley takes a fifty pence piece from his pocket and lays it on top of the pound notes. He makes no move towards actually placing the money in either of the Henshaws' hands. He smiles at them, benignly

Lumley Precisely the contrary, sir. It's always a pleasure to accommodate a customer. (*He pretends a sudden thought,* *raising a forefinger)* In fact . . . In fact, if I might venture a further suggestion.

Lumley beckons them to follow him across the shop. They do so, Mrs Henshaw casting backward glances at the money on the cash desk. Lumley picks up the jacket of the suit he originally tried on Henshaw

Yes, the Madison Avenue Executive suit. Exceptional value. An unbeatable bargain at the price. *(He detaches the maker's tag from the sleeve and proffers it to Henshaw)* Take this, sir.

Henshaw takes the tag and stares at it, blankly

Henshaw It's a price ticket.

Lumley Correction, sir. It's a sleeve tag. It contains not only the price but also the exact measurements of the suit: chest, waist, sleeve-length, outside-leg, inside-leg—I won't bore you with precise details.

Henshaw *(still mystified)* It belongs on that jacket.

Lumley My very best compliments to Mr Crisp Esquire, you'll find him in men's suiting at Messrs Brightlings. Present him with the sleeve tag. I sincerely hope and trust that he'll be able to accommodate you.

Mrs Henshaw takes the tag and examines it

Mrs Henshaw These measurements belong to that suit there.

Lumley Chest, waist, inside-leg, outside-leg, et cetera, et cetera.

Mrs Henshaw It didn't fit him.

Lumley *(with a supercilious smile)* Not without minor alterations, madam, as I've attempted to explain. Mr Henshaw is not a stock size. What we have there, I say what we have there is what's known in the trade as a thirty-eight short fitting garment. Allow me, sir.

Lumley unfastens the buttons of Henshaw's porter's jacket again and, before the railwayman knows what's happening, takes off his jacket once more

Mr Hartigan!

Hartigan steps forward. Lumley hands him the porter's jacket. Hartigan keeps a tight hold on it. Lumley picks up the jacket from the suit

Slip the jacket on again, sir. Just oblige me for my personal satisfaction.

Henshaw allows Lumley to help him into the jacket once again. Lumley takes a tailor's tape measure from around his neck and proceeds to take a few swift measurements of Henshaw, muttering to himself as he does so, approvingly. First, he measures Henshaw's back from the collar to the bottom of the jacket

Hm-hmmm. Allow me, sir.

Lumley extends Henshaw's arm and measures him from between the shoulder-blades to the tip of the sleeve cuff. Keeping Henshaw's arm raised, he bends the elbow, bringing the finger-tips across the chest, and measures the arm-length again

Hm-hmmmm. Allow me, sir.

Moving in front of Henshaw, Lumley slips the tape measure under the jacket and measures Henshaw's chest

Hm-hmmmm. Thank you.

Lumley marks the measurement of the tape with his thumb, removes the tape from Henshaw's chest and brandishes the measurement under Mrs Henshaw's nose

You see, madam! What can't speak can't lie! Mr Henshaw, to all intents and purposes, is a thirty-eight short to all and sundry in the tailoring profession.

Mrs Henshaw (*now bewildered*) But it doesn't *fit* him. Except where it touches.

Lumley Exactly. Mr Crisp at Brightlings *may*—I say, Mr Crisp might be able to accommodate you with a suit. (*He smiles, blandly*) But not without local alterations.

Mr and Mrs Henshaw exchange a doubtful glance

Henshaw What do you think then, Edith?
Mrs Henshaw I don't know. I don't know what to think. I'm in a quandary.

Lumley follows the above exchange with a polite smile. He moves forward

Lumley Allow me, sir. May I?

Lumley fastens the buttons on the jacket that Henshaw is wearing. He smooths the shoulders and steps back, approvingly. Henshaw raises an arm and gives the cloth a close look

Mrs Henshaw You see, I don't like that one—I'm not at all struck.

Henshaw No. I know. I can see you're not.

Lumley If I might venture a question, Mrs Henshaw? What is your precise objection to the suit? Is it the style? Is it the colour? Too loud is it?

Mrs Henshaw Well—yes.

Lumley Hm-hmmmm. (*He picks up a pattern book and riffles through it, selecting a cloth sample and showing it to Mrs Henshaw*) Something like that you had in mind, perhaps?

Mrs Henshaw studies the cloth carefully

Mrs Henshaw Yes. Something like that.

Lumley Yes. Hm-hmmm. You see, I can't do you that. It's bespoke, do you see? I say, I can't offer you that in a ready-to-wear suiting.

Mrs Henshaw I like that very much—I like it very much indeed, in fact.

Lumley takes hold of the pattern book again and runs a loving finger over the sample. A mammoth thought suddenly seems to strike him

Lumley Do—you—know—something! (*Calling to Hartigan*) Current order book, Mr Hartigan, on the double.

Hartigan collects the order book from the cash desk and brings it to Lumley who waits in silence with mounting excitement. Lumley takes the order book and studies it. He glances up, at last, with a knowing smile, looking from Mr Henshaw to Mrs Henshaw and back again

I thought I was right. JY three-four-two! (*He waits, as though expecting a reaction from the Henshaws but then, not getting one, continues*) You've selected the very same cloth as your good spouse, madam. JY three-four-two is the exact suiting which Mr Henshaw originally ordered!

Henshaw It is! That's it! I knew you'd like it, Edith, if you saw it!

Mrs Henshaw Oh.

Lumley Great minds think alike. And I have a further present-
ment regarding that particular material. Mr Hartigan, could I
trouble you for the delivery book?

*Hartigan gets the delivery book from the cash desk and brings it
to Lumley*

I may be wrong, and then I may be right, but that precise
pattern strikes a distinct chord in my memory. (*He studies the
book*) JY three-four-two. Unless I'm very sadly mistaken, sir,
the suit you ordered and I measured you for was delivered here
last night!

Henshaw You said six weeks it'd take—it's barely a month since
you measured me up for it.

Lumley We *say* six weeks, sir, in order not to disappoint the
customer. But it may be five, it could be four—it's dependant
upon expediency at Head Office. We never know. But a customer may require a suit for a specific occasion: a wedding,
an impending bereavement, we prefer to nominate six weeks
to defray the slight chance of disappointment. It's a company
ruling.

Mrs Henshaw (*wavering*) He's not having a suit made to measure.

Lumley I've already taken cognizance of your cancellation, Mrs
Henshaw. I merely remark upon the coincidence. You have come
here this morning to revoke an order which, by purest chance,
was almost certainly delivered only yesterday evening.

Mrs Henshaw Thirty-five pounds seventy-five for a suit for him,
it's ridiculous.

Lumley Madam, it's cancelled. Allow me, I say, allow me to
satisfy my curiosity. Mr Hartigan, pop into the fitting room
and ascertain as to whether or not delivery number eight-three-
five-six, pattern number JY three-four-two, consists of a suit
for our friend, Mr Henshaw, would you?

*Hartigan goes into the "fitting room"—a curtained cubicle, the
interior of which is visible to the audience. The cubicle contains a
full-length mirror, a chair, and a half-dozen or so bespoke suits
awaiting collection*

Lumley (*turning back to the Henshaws*) I stand to be corrected.

Henshaw If it is ready they've got their skates on with it!

Lumley (*with a modest smile*) They don't stand still, Mr Henshaw, at Head Office.

Lumley picks up Henshaw's porter's jacket, ostensibly to smooth out the creases but, in effect, to prevent Henshaw putting it on and leaving the shop

Excuse me, would you, just one brief moment?

Lumley, taking Henshaw's jacket with him, goes into the fitting room. He draws the curtain across the door so that the Henshaws cannot see in. Hartigan is still looking through the half-dozen suits, examining the sleeve tags. Lumley straightaway lifts a suit on a hanger from the rack

Allow me, Mr Hartigan. Order number eight-three-five-six, pattern number JY three-four-two, customer Henshaw. (*He hands the suit to Hartigan*)

Hartigan Did you know that was there when they walked in this morning?

Lumley smiles knowingly and detains Hartigan by the sleeve as he moves to leave the cubicle

Lumley Time, Mr Hartigan, time. In your own nomenclature we'll play it cool. (*He holds up the porter's jacket*) Brother Henshaw won't abscond. Allow him a moment to think things over with his good lady.

Lumley sits on the chair. He lights up a cigarette and takes a few hasty puffs, wafting away each puff of smoke with his free hand. Mr and Mrs Henshaw remain stiffly silent in the shop, feeling slightly uncomfortable

Henshaw What do you think then, Edith?
Mrs Henshaw You know what I think, Charles, I've had my say.
Henshaw I'm in two minds myself, I'm caught between two stools.

They lapse into silence again. In the fitting room, Lumley wafts away the smoke and continues

Lumley We may not be *au fait* with the modern trendy fal-de-rals, Mr Hartigan. I say we may not come to business in knitted ties and suède shoes, but we still have something to teach our younger associate in the matter of salesmanship. I say, we're not quite ready for the boneyard yet! (*He puts out his cigarette carefully, leaving no trace and putting the cigarette end in his top pocket, rises, and takes the suit from Hartigan*) Come on, MacDuff.

Lumley and Hartigan come out of the fitting room. Lumley carries the suit by its hanger. Hartigan is carrying Henshaw's porter's jacket

(*Cheerily*) I'm seldom in error, sir. I say, I'm seldom at fault. Something rang a bell somewhere. I have a memory bank like a technological computer, Mr—er—er—Henshaw.

Lumley displays the suit close to Henshaw's face, inviting him to touch it. Henshaw, unable to resist, feels the cloth

Henshaw Yes. Oh, yes. It's made up nice. Don't you think so?

But Mrs Henshaw refuses to be drawn

Lumley I'm particularly impressed with the fall of the lapels, speaking personally, of course.

Henshaw Oh, yes?

Lumley (*checking details*) Button two—yes. Jetted pockets—yes. Centre vent—yes. Inside pockets, two. I say, we can't fault our works' tailors on detail, can we?

Lumley allows Henshaw a quick glimpse of the lining and waistcoat, with the professional provocation of a strip-tease artist

Henshaw That'll be the waistcoat then, in there?

Lumley It will indeed. I wonder . . . (*He smiles and slips the jacket off the hanger*) I wonder if you'd do me a very great favour, sir? I'm wondering if you'd give me the personal satisfaction of seeing the jacket *on*?

Lumley holds up the jacket for Henshaw to slip his arms in the sleeves. Henshaw seeks his wife's approval

Mrs Henshaw There's nothing to stop you trying it on. Nothing at all.

Henshaw dives into the jacket. Lumley buttons it up, pulls down the jacket at the back, smooths the shoulders, and steps back appraisingly

Lumley (*modestly*) Hm-hmmmm. Hm-hmmmmm. Yes. Would
you do me a small favour, sir? Would you—just—walk about?

Henshaw takes the first, few, awkward and tentative steps

Lumley Would you permit me sir? (*He slips the tips of his fingers
underneath Henshaw's jacket lapels and runs them up and down,
for some apparently professional reason best known to himself.
He steps back*) Oh, yes! Oh, yes! My word, oh, yes!

Henshaw It is nice, isn't it?

Mrs Henshaw (*still not committing herself*) It's all right, for what
it is.

Lumley Mark you, madam, if it comes down to a question of
price, don't be influenced by me. You know best what you
yourselves can afford.

Mrs Henshaw (*sensing the implied insult*) It's not a question of
what we can or what we can't afford. We can afford what we
want. It's more a question of what we're going to pay. That's
what it's a question of.

Lumley If it's a question of value for money, madam. Satisfaction guaranteed . . .

Mrs Henshaw It's more a question of what we're satisfied *with*.

Lumley (*with a cold smile*) You have me at a loss?

Mrs Henshaw (*triumphantly*) The jacket's too short!

Henshaw Is it?

Mrs Henshaw Why, of course it is! Miles too short! You can
see it is—if you're not wearing it.

Lumley Ah! Ah! But just one moment, madam, and you'll
excuse the contradiction. The gentleman happens to be wearing
a different trouser. It's an optical illusion. A well-known
optical illusion to the trade. If the gentleman were wearing the
matching trouser, you'd have altogether a different effect.

Mrs Henshaw So you say.

Lumley Slip into the trousers, sir. To prove a point. (*He picks
up the hanger with the trousers and waistcoat and proffers them
to Henshaw*) Try them on.

Henshaw hangs back

Mr Hartigan! (*To Henshaw*) No compulsion, sir. No compulsion to buy at all. Just slip the waistcoat and the trousers on.

(To Hartigan, giving him the rest of the suit) Show Mr—er—Henshaw into our fitting room.

Hartigan This way, sir.

Hartigan sets off for the fitting room and Henshaw, with a hopeless shrug to his wife, follows him. Hartigan hangs the waistcoat and trousers on a hook in the fitting room and draws the curtain

Here we are, sir. If you'll just slip off the trousers you've got on . . .

Henshaw does so and gazes at his trouserless image in the full-length mirror. Then he puts on the suit. In the shop, Lumley does a brief but impressive tidying-up job, mostly for Mrs Henshaw's benefit, straightening a jacket-sleeve on a rack, altering the angle of a display shirt, removing a speck of dust. He returns, finally, to Henshaw's porter's jacket, picks it up, and folds it

Lumley The Royal Scot, the Flying Scotsman, the Master Cutler, they're all past history. The Master Cutler, correct me if I'm wrong, madam, I say, the Master Cutler was wont to journey from Sheffield to King's Cross in days of yore . . .

At this point, Henshaw, resplendent in the full suit, steps out of the fitting room. He is followed by Hartigan

My word! *(Smugly, to Mrs Henshaw)* I think I make my point, about the jacket length?

Henshaw approaches them, a little awkward at first, anxious for his wife's approval. Lumley, prepared to let the suit speak for itself, stands back, his hands clasped

Henshaw Well?

Mrs Henshaw Turn round.

Henshaw does so

Turn round again.

Again he obliges

I was wrong about the jacket, Charles. It's not too short.

Lumley *(indicating the mirror)* Sir? The back.

Henshaw examines himself over his shoulder

Sir? The walk again.

Again Henshaw walks about the shop, this time gaining confidence with ever step. The new suit has made a new man of him. His shoulders are pulled back, his stomach is drawn in, his chest is out. And even Mrs Henshaw is impressed

Mrs Henshaw It is, Charles, it really is—it's a lovely suit.

Henshaw moves close to his wife and they carry on their conversation in low tones. Lumley, respecting their domestic privacies, moves out of earshot

Henshaw You've changed your mind then, have you, about me having it?

Mrs Henshaw I haven't changed my mind, Charles, no.

Henshaw Well, what do you think?

Mrs Henshaw Well, I'm like you now, aren't I? I don't know what to think.

Henshaw But you like it now you've seen it on?

Mrs Henshaw I've said I like it. It's still a lot of money to lay out.

Henshaw Y'see, you've got to allow for the price of the waistcoat. With a two-piece suit, it might come cheaper—but with a two-piece job they don't chuck you a waistcoat in.

Mrs Henshaw I *know*. I know that, love. I'm just saying, it's a lot to lay out.

The Henshaws lapse into silence, considering the ins and outs of the matter. Lumley and Hartigan are also engaged in quiet conversation

Lumley Watch and learn, Mr Hartigan. I say, watch and learn and inwardly digest. Profit by example. We may pay regular visits to the barber, but we do have something to teach the younger generation. (*He becomes aware that the Henshaws are looking over towards him and he moves to join them, beaming*) How are we faring, all of us? Have we made our minds up, yet?

Mrs Henshaw (*with a nervous smile*) We were just saying, it's a lot of money to lay out.

Henshaw All in one go.

Lumley It is, it is. It's one of the reasons why Head Office, in their infinite wisdom, insist on a twenty per cent deposit as a general rule—a safeguard for the customer. (*He gives Henshaw a baleful glance*) We were prepared to bend the rules in your instance—ill-advisedly—let's hope events don't prove us wrong.

Henshaw preens, examines the jacket sleeves, clenching and unclenching his fists

Mrs Henshaw (*doubtfully*) Thirty-five pounds seventy-five. It's a lot to pay out.

Lumley Every satisfaction guaranteed.

Henshaw Less two-fifty, paid on.

Lumley Thirty-three twenty-five *in toto*.

Henshaw I haven't that much on me—I hadn't counted on taking it today.

Mrs Henshaw I could help you out.

Henshaw So you think I should?

Mrs Henshaw You *need* a suit. Your grey one's gone to the dogs. And if you did get a cheap one, off the peg, well, it might not wear, it might not last.

Henshaw It might not have a waistcoat.

Mrs Henshaw There's always that to be considered.

Henshaw With a pullover I don't feel properly dressed.

Lumley follows their conversation with an obsequious smile, switching his glance like a spectator at a tennis match. They pause

Lumley Are we in business, sir?

Henshaw I'll see what I've got.

Henshaw, forgetting that he is wearing the new jacket, feels in his inside pocket for his wallet. Lumley, recognizing his intent, hands him his porter's jacket

Henshaw Sorry! (*He examines the contents of his wallet*) Twenty-seven quid!

Mrs Henshaw (*examining the contents of her purse*) I can do you six.

Henshaw It'd leave you short.

Mrs Henshaw Well, it *would* leave me short. I'm not denying that.

Lumley If I might tender a suggestion—for established customers we are prepared to accept a cheque.

Mrs Henshaw He doesn't have a cheque-book.

Lumley Ah!

Mrs Henshaw He has a *bank* book. But he doesn't have cheques.

Lumley Unfortunate.

Henshaw I suppose we could leave the suit till later, call for it at the end of the month.

Lumley sucks his teeth, noisily. He cannot turn down the suggestion, but he is making it clear that he does not approve of the idea. Mrs Henshaw takes six pounds out of her purse and forces them on Henshaw

Mrs Henshaw Here.

Henshaw Are you sure?

Mrs Henshaw Don't argue—take it.

Lumley Sales book, Mr Hartigan.

Henshaw (*putting the wad of notes on the counter*) Thirty-three pounds——

Mrs Henshaw provides the loose change from her purse

—twenty-five pence.

Lumley Sales book, Mr Hartigan. (*To Henshaw*) Without wishing to influence you, sir, a wise decision. I say, you've done the right thing. An excellent choice of suiting and an excellent suit. (*He smooths the jacket shoulders again*) Oh, yes. A perfect fit. It's quite remarkable. Do you know, sir, I have been in the tailoring profession for thirty-seven years—apprentice, junior assistant, second sales, assistant manager at our Rochdale branch for many seasons—I've served a privileged term of service at Head Office—and I don't recall a better fitting suit in my entire career. I say, you've got one hundred and one per cent satisfaction there.

Hartigan hands Lumley the sales book

Thank you, Mr Hartigan. Make out the customer's balance of payment, would you?

Hartigan fills in the sales receipt at the counter as Lumley continues to extol the virtues of the suit

The shoulders, the back, the fall of the lapels, the collar—perfect (*Slipping his hands under Henshaw's armpits*) No tugging there? No? Oh, a beautifully fitting suit. You would find it difficult to get better satisfaction in a Saville Row establishment. I say, in London's West End they would require your presence at three or four fittings to obtain the identical overall effect. It really is remarkable.

Mrs Henshaw Take it off, Charles. Don't lounge about in it. Let him wrap it up for you.

Henshaw is about to remove the jacket

Lumley A moment, sir. Before you do. May I? Allow the artist a last look at his masterpiece. (*He steps back to appraise the suit again*) I may only have been the architect, I say I may have done no more than provide a working plan, but I claim my fair share of the credit. It really is unique value! I wonder if I might crave a favour of you, sir? I wonder—I say, I wonder if I might be allowed to *keep* the suit?

Henshaw Keep it?

Lumley Only until the luncheon hour, sir, don't be alarmed. To ensure absolute satisfaction—for my own peace of mind, not yours—I would like to have performed a minor alteration.

Mrs Henshaw What alteration? What's wrong with it?

Lumley Nothing, madam. Precisely my point. It's above reproach. To your husband and yourself that is a perfect suit. And rightly so. You are the public that we aim to please. I am a tailor. With my *professional* eye, I sense an eighth of an inch disparity in the right sleeve.

Mrs Henshaw Where?

Lumley Madam, you might examine the jacket underneath a microscope, and still be none the wiser. I am speaking as one who has spent a lifetime in the trade. Just for my own *personal* satisfaction I would like to have our local tailor re-dress the sleeve.

Mrs Henshaw Just a minute. Just stand back.

Lumley is suddenly nervous, sensing that he might have gone too far

Lumley (*moving between Henshaw and Mrs Henshaw*) There would be no charge for the service. Under the circumstances, I would see to it that Head Office undertook to defray the minimal cost.

Mrs Henshaw flaps a hand at Lumley, who is standing between herself and her husband

Mrs Henshaw Get back! Stand clear! Let the dog see the rabbit!

Lumley (*stepping back*) I assure you, madam, that what you see before you is a perfect fit! To the layman that's a faultless suit!

Mrs Henshaw (*ignoring Lumley*) It is, Charles. I *can* see it now. That right sleeve is longer than the left.

Lumley You *can not* see it, woman! It is not visible to the naked eye!

Mrs Henshaw Don't you adopt that tone of voice with me! I know what I can bloody see and what I can't!

Henshaw (*puzzled, lifting his arms and examining the sleeves*) Is it this one or is it that?

Mrs Henshaw It's that one, I can see very well which one it is!

Lumley The sleeves are identical! I was adopting a hypercritical turn of phrase!

Mrs Henshaw You were trying to foist him off with a suit that doesn't fit. We're not all wet behind the ears.

Hartigan (*proffering the sales book*) Balance of payment receipt, Mr Lumley.

Mrs Henshaw Never mind the balance of bloody receipt. Charles—take it off.

Lumley My good woman, if you'll allow me a moment to make my point . . .

Mrs Henshaw Charles, do as I say. Get in there and get it off.

Henshaw picks up his porter's jacket and ambles towards the fitting room. Lumley hesitates, unsure whether to pursue Henshaw or continue the argument with the wife

Lumley Sir—madam—sir . . .

Henshaw has gone into the fitting room. During the following he takes one last look at himself in the mirror, and then changes back into his railwayman's clothes. In the shop, Mrs Henshaw scoops up the money from the counter

Mrs Henshaw And while we're on the subject, there is his two pounds fifty pence deposit we'll have back.

Lumley Madam, may I just make a point . . .

Mrs Henshaw I don't want any argy-bargy, I want that money in my hand.

Lumley Madam, may I just . . .

Mrs Henshaw Because, if I haven't got it in my hand in two seconds flat I shall want to know the reason why.

Lumley *Madam.* If I might be allowed one word! With regard to the refund of cash deposits on cancellations Head Office policy is quite plain: the customer is credited with the requisite amount.

Mrs Henshaw How do you mean, credited?

Lumley That the amount in question, in your case two pounds fifty, shall be credited in your husband's name, and we have a firm Head Office ruling to that effect.

Mrs Henshaw Don't tell me about what Head Office says, because I shall get that money back if I have to go myself, personally, to your bloody Head Office, off my own bat. That two pounds fifty belongs to him and he wants it back. I shall go to the head man, whoever he is, I shall go to a solicitor if it comes to that.

Lumley Mrs Henshaw, try to understand. It's the simple equivalent to opening a credit account. For two pounds fifty. Then, in future, should your husband require a raincoat, a spring overcoat, anything of that nature, then he has the nucleus of a credit—with us.

Mrs Henshaw I'm not arguing. Are you going to give me that two pounds fifty or are you not?

They both look towards the fitting booth as Henshaw comes out. He is back in his railway uniform. His new found confidence is gone. His shoulders droop. His stomach sticks out. He is carrying the new suit and he lays it down, gently, ruefully, on the counter. Mrs Henshaw, Lumley and Hartigan all watch him in silence. After a moment he turns, breaking the mood

Henshaw Well then? Are we ready for off?

Mrs Henshaw We are—when I get that two pounds fifty back.

Henshaw (*to Lumley*) You'd better give it to her, mister. I'm due on shift.

Lumley picks up the two fifty he had previously placed on the cash desk and hands it to Mrs Henshaw, who takes it without a word

Many thanks.

Mrs Henshaw, followed by her husband, goes to the door. Henshaw pauses at the door and speaks without rancour

Henshaw All the very best.

Mr and Mrs Henshaw go out

Lumley glares at Hartigan, who pretends to work. Lumley paces the shop, officiously re-aligning a display shirt and an array of ties. It is some moments before Hartigan dares venture a comment

Hartigan You slipped up there, Mr Lumley. You'd sold him that suit. You got carried away. You went over the top.

Lumley does not reply or even look at Hartigan. For some moments he seems lost in thought. At last, he turns and snaps

Lumley I had cause to observe earlier this morning that the ready-to-wear stock is acquiring dust. Elbow-grease, Mr Hartigan. Apply some elbow-grease with a whisk! Head Office are not inclined to give us prior notice before they descend upon us. And you might make mental note about coming to work properly dressed. I say, in our profession, a dark grey figured tie is considered correct.

Lumley stalks across to the plate-glass door and stares out into the street. Hartigan picks up a tailor's whisk and begins his task of brushing down the entire ready-to-wear stock. He seems cheerful enough though; he is whistling, as—

the CURTAIN *slowly falls*

FURNITURE AND PROPERTY LIST

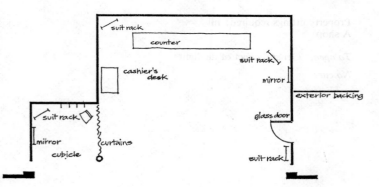

On stage: Long counter. *On it:* display shirts, ties and other men's clothing. *On shelves below:* pattern books of cloth pieces, rolls of cloth, tailor's whisk

Cashier's desk. *On it:* order books, sales books, delivery books, writing materials

Wall mirror

Around walls: ready-to-wear suits on racks

Fitting cubicle. *In it:* mirror, rack with bespoke suits on hangers, hooks, chair

Personal: **Lumley:** wallet with 2 pound notes, coins including fifty pence piece, tape measure, cigarettes, matches

Henshaw: wallet with 27 pound notes

Mrs Henshaw: purse with 6 pound notes and loose coins

LIGHTING PLOT

Property fittings required: nil
A shop

To open: General effect of daylight

No cues